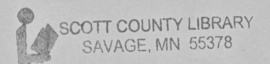

Looking at Minibeasts

Ants, Bees, and Wasps

Sally Morgan

Thameside Press

Contents

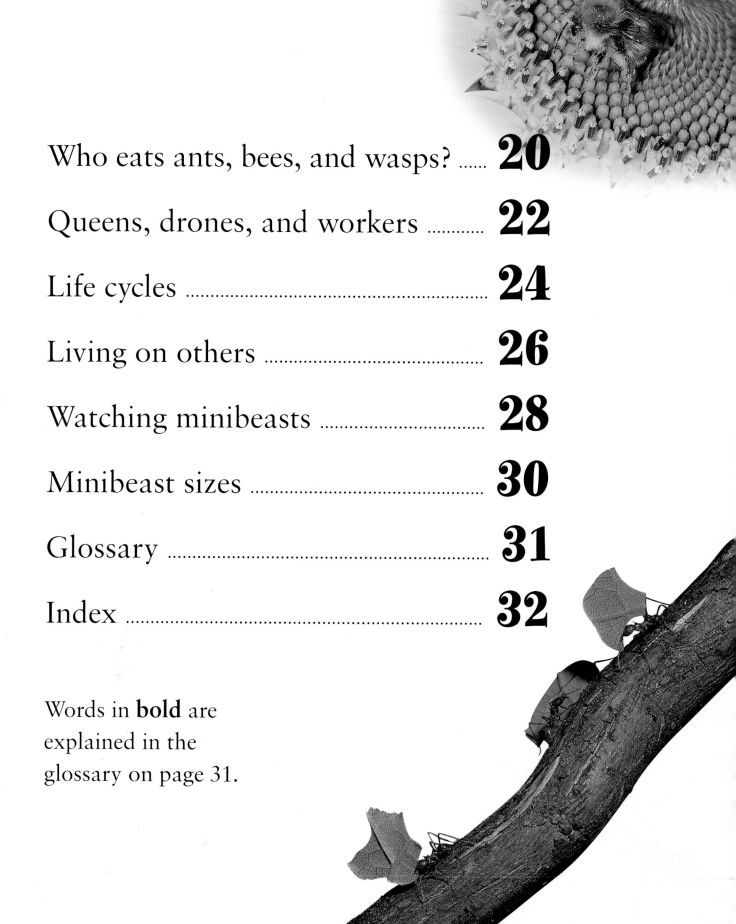

Words in **bold** are
explained in the
glossary on page 31.

What are ants, bees, and wasps?

Ants, bees, and wasps are **insects**. Insects have a body made up of three parts—a head, a **thorax**, and an **abdomen**. They all have six legs. There are three legs on each side of the body. The head has two eyes and a pair of **antennae**.

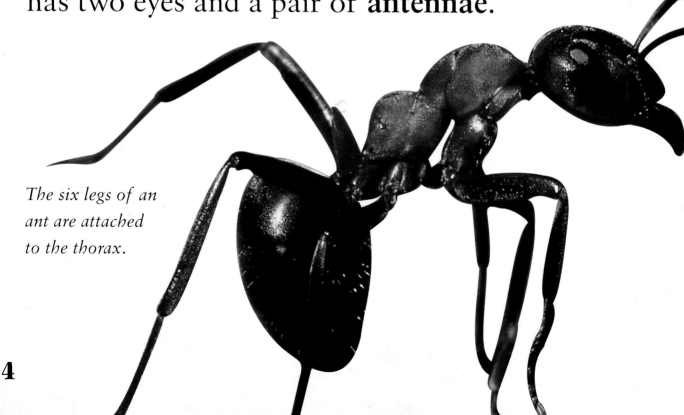

The six legs of an ant are attached to the thorax.

The buzz of a bee is made by the beating of its wings.

Bees and wasps have two pairs of wings, which are attached to their thorax. But ants are wingless for most of their life. Unlike other insects, ants, bees, and wasps have a "waist" between their thorax and abdomen.

Wasps have two pairs of thin wings, which are almost see-through.

5

The bee family

There are more than 100,000 different types of ants, bees, and wasps. These insects are found all around the world. They range in size from tiny ants, which are barely a fraction of an inch long, to giant wasps and hornets, which are several inches long.

Hornets are large wasps that catch caterpillars to feed their young.

Not all wasps are black and yellow in color. This digger wasp is a shiny black.

The most common bee is the honeybee. There are also bumblebees and bees that live on their own. There are large hornets with a painful sting, **parasitic** wasps that lay their eggs in or on other animals, and sawflies, which are tiny wasps.

Weaver ants live and work together.

Living together

Most ants, bees, and wasps live in large groups called **colonies**. Each member of the colony has a job to do. Some hunt for food, while others look after the young in the nursery. The number of insects living together can be huge.

*These ants are looking after eggs and **pupae** in the nursery.*

There can be up to 100,000 ants living in one nest.

This swarm of bees will find a place where they can build a new nest.

Some bees and wasps are called solitary, which means they live alone. Solitary wasps make small nests in the soil or in holes in walls.

Solitary wasps live by themselves, not in a group. They make a burrow in which they lay their eggs.

Building a home

Wild bees make their nests in hollow trees or old buildings. Inside a nest are rows of cells called a **honeycomb**. Honeycomb is made from wax, which a worker bee produces from its abdomen. It kneads it into shape with its strong jaws.

*Most honeybees live in **hives** owned by beekeepers.*

Inside, worker bees fill the honeycomb with honey.

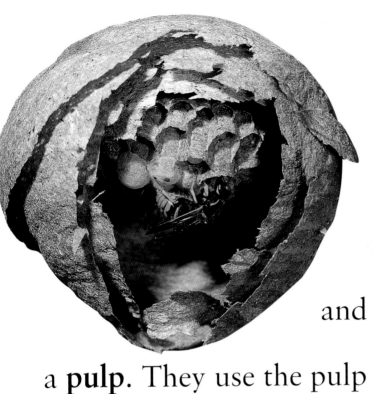

The tree wasp's nest is made up of layers that cover the cells inside.

Wasps collect wood from logs and fences and chew the fibers into a **pulp**. They use the pulp to make their paper-like nests. The common wasp makes its nest underground in burrows left by small animals. Tree wasps make nests in hollow trees and in the attics of houses.

The nest grows bigger as the worker wasps add more layers to the outside.

Where do ants live?

Ants live in nests. Garden ants like to build their nests in warm, dry places, such as under paving stones or near walls. A maze of tunnels leads into the underground chamber where the ants lay their eggs.

Some ants build a nest under a mound of leaves and twigs.

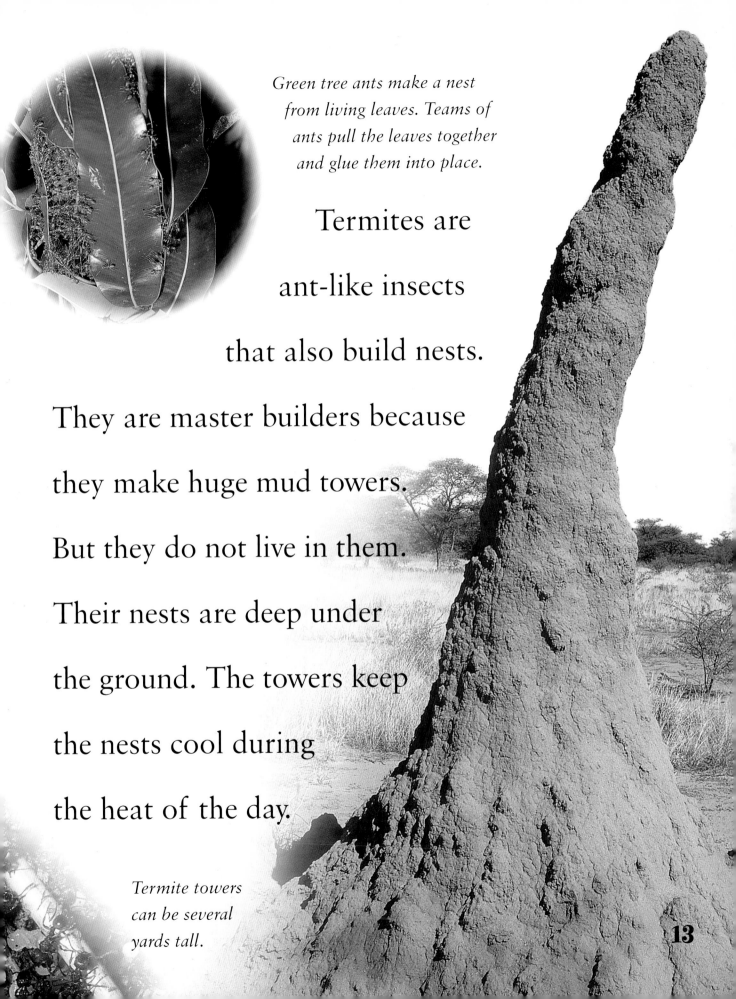

Green tree ants make a nest from living leaves. Teams of ants pull the leaves together and glue them into place.

Termites are ant-like insects that also build nests. They are master builders because they make huge mud towers. But they do not live in them. Their nests are deep under the ground. The towers keep the nests cool during the heat of the day.

Termite towers can be several yards tall.

What do bees and wasps eat?

A bee's favorite food is the **nectar** of flowers. Bees have a tongue-like **proboscis** that they use to suck up the nectar. They store nectar in their stomachs

This bumblebee is sucking up nectar. Its proboscis is hidden among the petals.

and take it back to the **hive,** where it is made into honey. Bees also collect pollen from flowers and place it in special pockets on their back legs.

Bees carry pollen back to their hive to feed their larvae.

Wasps like sugary foods, too. They are attracted to soft drinks and jelly. But a wasp **larva** needs meat. In the early summer, wasps hunt for caterpillars and aphids to feed their young.

In the early fall, wasps sip the juice from fallen fruits.

Finding flowers

Bees are experts at finding flowers. Their eyes can see colors that our eyes cannot. Many flowers have black marks, invisible to our eyes, called guide lines. These lines lead the bees to the nectar.

This is how we see a dandelion.

This is how a bee sees a dandelion.

Bees may go on up to sixteen trips from the hive each day, and each one may last an hour or more.

A bee may visit as many as a thousand flowers on an outing from its hive.

When a bee returns to the hive it tells the others where to find the flowers by doing a dance. The type of dance tells the bees whether the food is nearby or farther away.

Hunting for food

Every day, ants leave the nest in search of food. They hunt for dead animals that they can carry back to the nest. If the animal is too large, they bite off small pieces of it. Some ants can kill small animals by biting them to death.

Army ants are swarming over this cockroach. They will rip it to pieces and carry it back to their nest.

Aphids produce a sugary waste called honeydew that ants collect and take back to their nest.

Ants love sugary foods. They feed on the nectar from flowers, the honeydew from aphids, and even sugar in the kitchen.

Leafcutter ants carry small pieces of leaf back to their underground nests.

Who eats ants, bees, and wasps?

Ants are a favorite food for many animals. The anteater uses its powerful claws to dig into a termite nest. Then it pushes its long, sticky tongue inside. It eats thousands of termites in a day.

The giant anteater has a good sense of smell, which it uses to find termite nests.

A bee-eater eats bees, wasps, and other insects. It beats a bee's body against its perch to remove the stinger. This makes the bee safe to eat.

Few animals eat bees and wasps because they have a painful sting. The black and yellow colors are a warning to other animals to stay away. A bee or wasp will defend itself by stinging its attacker. Once a bee has used its stinger, it dies.

The honey badger's thick fur protects it from bee stings. It rips open bees' nests with its claws and licks up the honey.

Queens, drones, and workers

There may be as many as 50,000 bees living in a single hive. Most of them are worker bees, which live for only four or five weeks. Worker bees build, clean, and repair the hive, look after the young, and hunt for food.

A queen bee (marked with a white spot) may lay as many as 2,000 eggs in a single day.

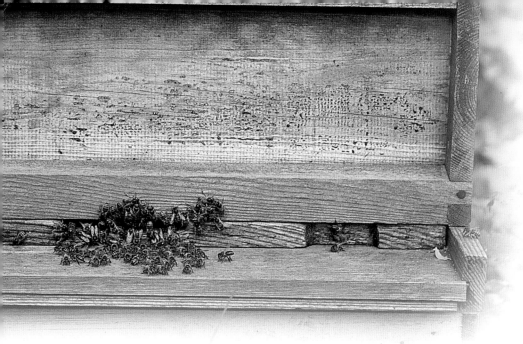

Some worker bees act as guards at the entrance to the hive. They protect the hive and help keep it cool by fanning air with their wings.

Workers are female, but they cannot lay eggs. Only one female can lay eggs, and that is the queen bee. She may live for up to five years and is much larger than the other bees. There are a few male bees called **drones**.

A termite queen is huge. Worker termites look after her while she lays thousands of eggs.

Life cycles

Bees spend the winter in their hives, where they eat their store of food. In the spring, the queen bee starts egg-laying. An egg hatches into a larva. The larva is fed on honey and pollen so that it grows quickly. After a few weeks, the larva turns into a **pupa**. Inside the pupal case, the larva changes into an adult bee.

This young worker bee is crawling out of her pupal case. The hairs on her body and her wings are still damp.

During the pupal stage, the body of the bee larva changes as it becomes an adult.

If the hive becomes too crowded, some of the eggs develop into new queens. A swarm of bees leaves the hive with a queen. This swarm builds a new nest with their own queen.

In the late summer, winged ants called flying ants fly away from the nest to form a new colony.

Living on others

Some wasps live by themselves, so they have to find a safe place to lay their eggs. Many wasps lay their eggs in tiny pots that they make from sand or mud. They put a small animal inside the pot together with their egg. When the wasp larva hatches it feeds on the body of the animal.

The potter wasp makes a mud pot. She pushes a caterpillar into the pot together with an egg. When the wasp larva hatches, it feeds on the caterpillar.

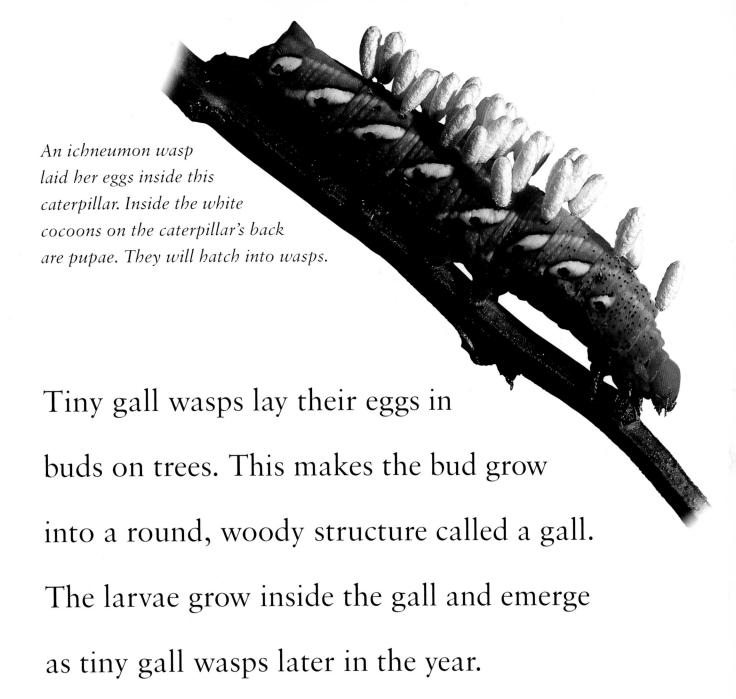

An ichneumon wasp laid her eggs inside this caterpillar. Inside the white cocoons on the caterpillar's back are pupae. They will hatch into wasps.

Tiny gall wasps lay their eggs in buds on trees. This makes the bud grow into a round, woody structure called a gall. The larvae grow inside the gall and emerge as tiny gall wasps later in the year.

The velvet ant hunts out the nests of bumblebees and lays its eggs on the bee larvae.

Watching minibeasts

Ants, bees, and wasps can all be seen in gardens and parks during the summer months.

Watch how bees move from flower to flower collecting nectar and pollen. How long do they spend at each flower? Do they visit every flower or just a few? Do they come back to a flower again?

Bees will soon find the sugary water placed on colored cardboard cirlces.

To find out which color is a bee's favorite, place colored cardboard circles (about the size of a saucer) on a sunny lawn near some flowers. Dribble some sugary water in the center of each card. Watch to see which color the bees fly to first.

Lift the stone up carefully so you don't disturb the ants too much.

Ants often make their nest under stones. Find a warm, sunny spot and place an old paving stone on the ground. Go back a few weeks later and see if ants have nested underneath. If you lift the stone you may be able to see the tunnels, eggs, and pupae of the ants.

Many trees and shrubs, especially oak trees, have galls caused by gall wasp larvae. Inside a gall there are hollow spaces called chambers. Open up a gall to see if you can find a larva inside.

Knobbly round growths on oak trees contain gall wasp larvae.

Warning: Don't go too close to bees or wasps, because they can sting.

Minibeast sizes

Ants, bees, and wasps are many different sizes. The pictures in this book do not show them at their actual size. Below you can see how big some of them are in real life.

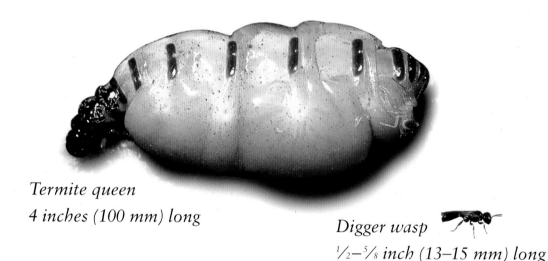

Termite queen
4 inches (100 mm) long

Digger wasp
¹/₂–⁵/₈ inch (13–15 mm) long

Wood ant
¹/₂ inch (10 mm) long

Wasp
⁷/₈ inch (22 mm) long

Bumblebee
⁵/₈ inch (16 mm) long

Glossary

abdomen The rear or back part of an insect's body.

antennae The feelers on an insect's head.

colonies Large groups of insects living together.

drones The male bees in a colony.

hive A place where honeybees live and rear young.

honeycomb A wax structure made by bees in a hive to store honey, eggs, and larvae.

insect An animal with six legs and three parts to its body.

larva A young insect. It looks very different to the adult.

nectar The sugary liquid made by flowers.

parasitic Living on another living animal.

proboscis (say: *pro-boss-iss*) A long mouthpart for piercing or sucking food.

pulp A soft mass.

pupa A hard case made from the skin of a larva.

thorax The middle part of an insect's body, between the head and the abdomen.

Index

U.S. publication copyright © 2001 Thameside Press

International copyright reserved in all countries.
No part of this book may be reproduced in any
form without written permission from the publisher.

Distributed in the United States by
Smart Apple Media
1980 Lookout Drive
North Mankato, MN 56003

Text by Sally Morgan
Illustrations by Woody

Editors: Claire Edwards, Sue Barraclough
Designer: John Jamieson
Picture researcher: Sally Morgan
Educational consultant: Emma Harvey

ISBN: 1-930643-10-1

Printed in Hong Kong

9 8 7 6 5 4 3 2 1

Library of Congress Cataloging-in-Publication Data

Morgan, Sally.
   Ants, bees, and wasps / Sally Morgan.
     p. cm. -- (Looking at minibeasts)
     ISBN 1-930643-10-1
     1. Hymenoptera--Juvenile literature. [1. Ants. 2. Bees.
3. Wasps.] I. Title.

   QL565.2 .M67 2001
   595.79--dc21

                                    2001023452

Picture acknowledgments: Ian Beames/Ecoscene: 24. Antony
Cooper/Ecoscene: 21b. Peter Currell/Ecoscene: 4, 30bl. Michael
Gore/Ecoscene: 20. Simon Grove/Ecoscene: 27b. Alexandra
Jones/Ecoscene: 13t. Neeraj Misha/Ecoscene: 21t. Papilio:
front & back cover tcl, tr, cl & cr, 1, 2, 3t, 3b, 5t, 5b, 9t, 11t,
11b, 12, 15t, 15b, 16cl, 16br, 17t, 19b, 25t, 30bc, 30br. K.G.
Preston-Mafham/Premaphotos: 8, 13r, 18, 26. R.A. Preston-
Mafham/Premaphotos: 23t. Kjell Sanders/Ecoscene: front &
back cover tl, 7b, 23b, 27t, 30c. Alan Towse/Ecoscene: 10b, 22.
Barry Webb/Ecoscene: 10bl. Robin Williams/Ecoscene: front
& back cover tcr, front cover c, 6, 7t, 9b, 14t, 19t, 25b, 30cr.